SCHIRMER'S LIBRARY OF MUSICAL CLASSICS

FERDINAND SIEBER

Thirty-Six Eight-Measure Vocalises

For Elementary Vocal Teaching

IN SIX EDITIONS

➔ For Soprano (Op. 92) — Library Vol. 111

For Mezzo-Soprano (Op. 93) — Library Vol. 112

For Alto (Op. 94) — Library Vol. 113

For Tenor (Op. 95) — Library Vol. 114

For Baritone (Op. 96) — Library Vol. 115

For Bass (Op. 97) — Library Vol. 116

ISBN 978-0-7935-8826-8

G. SCHIRMER, *Inc.*

DISTRIBUTED BY

HAL•LEONARD®
CORPORATION

7777 W. BLUEMOUND RD. P.O. BOX 13819 MILWAUKEE, WI 53213

Elementary Vocalises
for
Soprano.

FERD. SIEBER. Op. 92.

N. B. All the exercises are to be sung, at first, on various vowels (a, o, e), and, later, on the syllables written under them. Do *not* observe, at first, the directions given for shading, but execute each exercise in a quiet, smooth *piano*, and as *legato* as possible. The tempo to be employed depends on the needs and the ability of the singer. At every rest, and at the breathing-marks (✛), breath *must* be taken; it *may* also be taken (if necessary) at the commas (ʼ).

14681

13.

14.

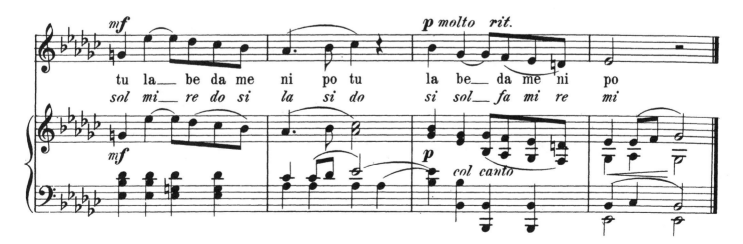

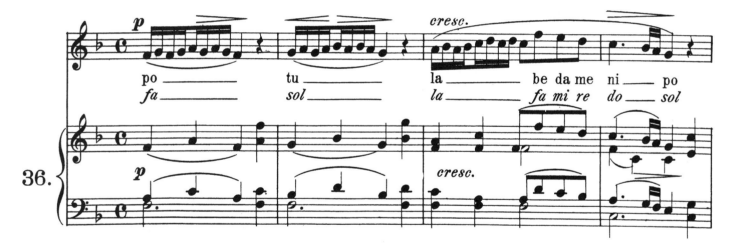